A Legacy Created

A Legacy Created

⋖ Memoir of a Boy from the South ⋗

by *Thomas Benson* III

A Legacy Created

Published by Wisdom House Books, Inc.
Chapel Hill, North Carolina 27516 USA
1.919.883.4669 | www.wisdomhousebooks.com

Wisdom House Books is committed to excellence in the publishing industry.

Book design copyright © 2021 by Wisdom House Books, Inc. All rights reserved.

Cover and Interior Design by Ted Ruybal

Published in the United States of America

Paperback ISBN: 978-0-578-89003-6
LCCN: 2021906856

1. BIO002010 | BIOGRAPHY & AUTOBIOGRAPHY /
Cultural, Ethnic & Regional / African American & Black

2. BIO026000 | BIOGRAPHY & AUTOBIOGRAPHY / Personal Memoirs

3. BIO019000 | BIOGRAPHY & AUTOBIOGRAPHY / Educators

First Edition

25 24 23 22 21 20 / 10 9 8 7 6 5 4 3 2 1

Table of Contents

Dedication

To my family and friends in the town of Lyman,
South Carolina, who loved, supported, and guided me
through this life journey.

Chapter One

The Sight of that Old Creepy House

During the early seventies, the time was one of trials and tribulations. In many ways, the period was a time where women, blacks, Native Americans, gays, and lesbians were marginalized people who were fighting for equality and a time where many people were against the Vietnam war. Life in rural South Carolina was slow, and the family was more precious than gold. Black Americans were in a state of struggle. A struggle for equal rights and a struggle for financial stability. Families bonded together and shared both moments of suffering and moments of joy. Families cared for each other and neighborhood families looked out for the kids in the neighborhood to ensure that everyone was safe.

I was just five years old when my mother decided a week before my fifth birthday that she would need to go back to work to help make ends meet in the household. My mom and dad agreed that my great aunts Linnie and Pat would babysit while they worked. These ladies were the mothers of the family. If someone needed food, money, shelter, or warm words of encouragement they were there with open arms.

The night before my mom would be leaving me to begin her first day of work, I put my hands together to begin my conversation with a nightly prayer as I knew that my mom would be leaving soon. I was so afraid—uncertain about how I'd feel being left alone and my mom not being in what I considered my everyday routine of seeing her there when I came home. The many times I smelled fresh corn and okra frying on the stove made me awfully excited. In life, one must accept change not as a challenge but as an opportunity to redefine the norm of routine. You see, I was someone who loved the presence of my mom. Morning would come too soon, and I wasn't ready for this new experience. My mom yelled, "Wash up and get ready to go!" She prepared cereal and orange juice for me before we left.

My mom and I were on our way to Aunt Linnie's. My aunts lived only five minutes away from our house. As we drove along the dirt road leading up to Aunt Linnie's, all I could see from my back seat windows were trees that enclosed the dirt trail leading up to the house. The closer we got to the home, the more frightened I became. The house from a distance was menacing with old worn weathered white wood and many tree limbs hung over and around the white weathered house. The house served as refuge for many out-of-town guests and kinfolk. I became more comfortable with the house after the warm greeting that I received from my Aunt Linnie. She was wearing a white dress, with a white scarf wrapped around her head. Her face was warm and gentle. She had a soft-spoken voice, and a look of wisdom embodied her presence.

A draw well, which was said to provide water that granted special powers to those who drank from it, sat on a concrete slab near the house. A gigantic tree with green banana shape buds sat in the front yard with branches that stretched out like two giant hands. Also, in the front yard grew a unique bush that was the topic of many discussions for young inexperienced parents, called the "switch tree." The switch was a device used for providing youngsters discipline and was notoriously known for stinging the hind parts of stubborn or unruly kids. The "switch" could be a long or short piece of bark, sometimes with thorns, but mostly thin bark. If your parents had a switch, it was Mother Nature's way of helping parents assist their kids with discipline. Discipline for any offense that went against what a parent's directive was. It seemed as if every switch that was removed from this tree was the perfect disciplinary device.

A chicken coop sat at the side of the house where my great aunts raised their chicks. Many of the chicks grew to become chickens and roosters roaming around in the yard. Behind the back of the house, just down the hill sat the outhouse. Rumors had been passed down from one generation to the other about the dangers that lurked inside the outhouse.

One day during my stay at my aunts', I had eaten a whole box of prunes not knowing that they would upset my stomach while waiting for my mom to pick me up. The unfortunate thing was that I had eaten so many prunes that after a while, my stomach could not contain it anymore. So, when my mom arrived, I pleaded with her to leave so that I could use the toilet at home. My mom talked, talked, and talked until she completely forgot about my desire to use the restroom. While my mom continued to talk endlessly, I decided to run down to the outhouse. I slowly peeked inside the toilet shed, and as my fear grew, the stronger my urge was to poop. I slowly stepped inside, and the smell of rotten eggs and old mildewed wood made my stomach turn even worse. I then lifted the toilet lid, and to my amazement, I noticed larvae, worms, and something bubbling inside the toilet. As I battled the urge within my stomach, I dripped with sweat from the fear of having to sit on the toilet. I slowly pulled my pants down, and as I moved to sit on the toilet, I noticed something strange.

As I looked down into the toilet, I began to observe the contents within the toilet moving slowly towards me and the bubbling grew louder as I sat. But because I had eaten so many plums, I could not stop "going." When my mother finally realized that I was missing, she walked down to the outhouse. As she opened the door, she realized that I was standing in maggot infested water, poop, and other disgusting things. She frantically tried to assist me, but with little success. I will forever be scarred by the notorious outhouse. And from that day on, I never stepped back into the outhouse. I would take a squat beside the outhouse once or twice, but I was never going back into there.

When anyone entered my Aunt Linnie's house, the screen door made a weird high-pitched noise that became louder as the door slammed shut. Rumors spread that an older cousin had received a broken finger from moving too slowly as the door shut.

The front porch of the house sat high over a steep hill that overlooked a small river stream. The front porch also was the place where during the mid-summer months my aunts and their guests would sit and converse for hours at a time. I remember one evening as the sun went down how amazing it was to see the flickering lightning bugs and the smell of honeysuckles. I always liked to see the flickering lightning bugs because they illuminated the dark sky, and it was fun to catch them with your hand and watch the tails of these bugs illuminate.

I knew that my new surroundings would be exciting and challenging all at the same time, but I would make the best of my situation even though I was genuinely going to miss my mother. I gave my mother a firm hug and kiss, and away she went on her first day back to work. I fought back the tears, because I knew my mother would be sad if she observed me crying. Aunt Linnie gave a final wave of goodbye to my mother as she drove away. She hugged me and told me that I would be okay, and before I could blink an eye, my mother would be back to pick me up at the end of the day.

Chapter Two

The Excitement of the Cotton Field

Living in the South during the early seventies was unique, because cotton fields were still prevalent and many areas in the South were still farming cotton fields and tobacco. Many times, I got the opportunity to assist my Aunt Linnie and Aunt Pat with their jobs of picking cotton from their cotton field. Aunt Linnie, Aunt Pat, and Uncle LJ were three family members of a larger family living a life without the modern necessities that most families were accustomed to. They raised their cows to make their milk and butter. They did not believe in taking their money to the banks because they did not trust giving their hard-earned money over to someone in an institution. They did not own a car, nor did they hold driver's licenses. Society changed, but they refused to assimilate with it.

Aunt Linnie and Aunt Pat were descendants of wealthy landowners who loved clothing, furniture, and jewelry.

Many of their belongings were heirlooms passed down from one generation to the next. Aunt Linnie and Pat made much of their money through cotton and doing little jobs for people around the town. I had never seen cotton before, so during the mornings they would grab their cotton bags, and along they would go to the cotton field. I loved my new job of transporting Aunt Linnie's cotton bag or monitoring my Great Uncle LJ while they attended the cotton field.

Uncle LJ was a veteran of World War II, and during his time in World War II, he was left disabled due to his injuries suffered while serving in the war. I would hold my Uncle LJ's hand and guide him around the cotton field while Aunt Linnie and Pat completed their jobs in the field. I had never seen a cotton field, so this was quite an exciting moment for me. I carefully inspected the cotton bud and realized that it resembled a rose, except for the white cotton sprouting from the stem. As a little boy, I learned the value of work and the commitment to family. My small role of ushering Uncle LJ through the cotton field allowed me the opportunity of creating my own relationship with my great uncle and I had a sense of duty to him, which was wonderful as a little boy.

My Aunt Linnie and I would always come from the cotton field and retrieve a metal dipper, which was kept by the sink. This metal dipper provided a quick sip from the sink in the kitchen. It never mattered how warm the weather was outside; this metal dipper always made the water from the sink seem extra cold. I loved to hold the cup by its handle and taste the refreshing cold water quench my thirst. Many times, I would drink so much water that I would lose my appetite for food. And Aunt Linnie was the most excellent cook. She could always prepare the tastiest meals.

Chapter Three

Wisdom in the Pictures

Pictures mean so much to so many people. Back in the seventies, most homes had pictures of President John F. Kennedy, Reverend Martin Luther King Jr., or the most common picture was that of the white Jesus. The pictures helped guide us through time periods where our societies were at crossroads with racism and moments of change for our people. Most families had the picture of Jesus because it symbolized strength, faith, hope, and love. Black Americans have always believed that their strength has come from their belief in Jesus.

Reverend Martin Luther King Jr. symbolized the fight for equal rights for all Black Americans and how people of all races should come together and love one another. John F. Kennedy sympathized for the Black American people and supported the struggle for equal rights. He had a strong relationship with Martin Luther King Jr. and together they fought for the rights of Black Americans. Pictures also have been a reflection for me to look back into moments in my life, as I have struggled to make the most out of my life experiences. Some are good and some are bad.

One morning I woke up bright and early and the sky was gloomy when I arrived at my Aunt Linnie's. As my mother drove away, Aunt Linnie grabbed my hand and escorted me into the house where *Captain Kangaroo* was on television. She laid me softly on the bed, where I slept until breakfast was ready. As I awoke, I jumped down from the bed and looked at the old pictures that hung in the living room. One picture looked like a green pasture where the morning dew had settled. The picture's color and texture were so realistic that I envisioned myself running through the foggy meadow. The other picture hanging over the bed in the living room was creepy. This picture showed the face of an older woman with grayish hair. Her eyes were brown, and they seemed to follow you as you moved farther away. I noticed the lime green dress that the lady wore. I wondered why the lady had such a gloomy, mysterious face. I thought maybe she was sad or depressed.

Aunty Linnie yelled for me to come into the kitchen and eat breakfast. As I walked into the kitchen, I noticed the floor crackling as I made each step toward the kitchen door. As I entered the adjoining bedroom, I saw a black man's picture with a distinguished look upon his face. The man wore a black church suit with a white dress shirt and a brownish necktie. The man's face had a glimpse of despair and deep sadness. As I stared at the picture, my Aunt Linnie entered the adjoining room and noticed me.

Aunt Linnie began to tell me the story of the man in the picture. She said he was a civil rights leader who fought for the rights and privileges of black people and how he was a great man. She told me that I could one day be a strong black man like the man in the picture. She told me the man in the picture was Martin Luther King Jr. Aunt Linnie explained to me how black people could not take many photos, and if they were fortunate enough to have money, they would have self-portraits made of themselves. She stated that she received that photo as a gift, and she wanted all guests to honor and respect the man in the picture.

Chapter Four

Courage and Confidence

Robbie was the nephew of my mom and my mom's sister's son. He was the first-born grandson of my grandfather and grandmother. Robbie was a year older than me, and he was very confident and courageous. When I arrived at my Aunt Linnie's, my older cousin, Robbie, was there, and he was very comfortable being at our aunt's house. Aunt Linnie and Pat always made the best biscuits and my cousin and I would eat them alone without anything else. They were always very moist and soft. You could eat three biscuits and never need a drink of water.

Robbie brought a bag full of small cars with him when he came, and I was astonished by the number of cars he had inside the bag, also how he knew the model of each car. He shared several cars with me, and we played on the floor until lunchtime. Robbie was adventurous and was not afraid to venture anywhere outside. He and I would walk down to the creek to watch the water flow over the rocks. Running, jumping, hiding, and playing like there was no tomorrow is what we enjoyed every day. We savored the moment of grabbing the cold water dipper to get a quick drink of water. We challenged each other in many of the different games we would play. One game we played often consisted of each of us taking turns peeing across the dirt driveway. The goal was to see whose pee could reach the farthest. Many times, it was a back-and-forth challenge that depended on how far you could bend your back backwards and how strong you could force your pee to go. We also challenged each other in spitting contests and that was always fun and exciting.

Robbie taught me many valuable lessons during our time together at Aunt Linnie's. I learned to be confident and courageous. During our time together he showed me how to be confident in myself and my abilities and to not allow fear to impede me. Throughout my life, there have been many times where my confidence and courage have propelled me to greater opportunities. Life is full of challenges that are unforeseen; therefore, we must learn to believe in ourselves and have the courage of a fighter.

Chapter Five

Saturday Ritual

F riday nights were special, but it was always assuring to me when I could wake up on Saturdays and watch all the great cartoons on television. I would normally grab a bowl and my favorite cereal and sit alone in front of the television mesmerized and excited about what programs were about to come on. Saturdays were the best because I would wake up early and watch *The Bugs Bunny Road Runner Hour, Scooby Doo Where are You? The Shazam/Isis Hour, Valley of the Dinosaurs,* and *Fat Albert and the Cosby Kids.* Those shows were the best! You could always laugh and find something interesting to share with others about the shows. My mom would start her Saturday cleaning ritual, which would often include me pitching in to help with taking the trash out, dusting, or any other cleaning objective she had in mind. Sometimes she would take a break to share in the laughs with me especially when *The Bugs Bunny Road Runner Show* was on. We would often laugh together about how Bugs Bunny was so much smarter than other characters.

The Road Runner always amazed me. He was smart, clever, and fast. The Coyote was no match for Road Runner. I sometimes wished that the Coyote could have caught the Road Runner at times because he never got a break. Cartoons back then meant a lot to kids. They entertained us for hours and often had a moral point at the end of the show. My Saturday morning ritual was heartwarming to me because it allowed me to let all the craziness of the week to be forgotten and gave me the opportunity to be a kid. I was able to learn how to deescalate my emotions from the week and disappear into the television programming that played on Saturdays. That ritual is still important to me today, but unfortunately the programming isn't the same.

Chapter Six

Going to Sunday School

I was taught at an early age that Sundays were dedicated to the Lord, and that we should rest and give honor to our God. Our commitment to God who gives us strength is engrained in me, therefore every Sunday must be a sacred day for giving honor to our Lord and Savior. It was always sad when Saturday night came around because every Sunday I had to go to Sunday school and then church. My mom was relentless about attending those services. She would always tell me if I could wake up on Saturday and watch television and play all day, it was an expectation that my behind was going to be in Sunday school and church.

Sunday school was not bad, but I would have preferred to sleep in. My mom would always dress me in the nicest clothes and shoes. It always began with everyone sitting in the main part of the church and someone would start with a hymn and others would follow in the hymnal. After the hymnal the very few people attending Sunday school would have a general discussion about the church service, a prayer would occur, and then someone would be designated to say the Lord's Prayer:

> *Our Father who art in heaven, hallowed be thy name. Thy kingdom come. Thy will be done. On earth as it is in heaven. Give us this day our daily bread. And forgive us our trespasses. As we forgive those who trespass against us. And lead us not into temptation. But deliver us from evil. For thine is the kingdom, and the power, and the glory, for ever and ever. Amen.*

I still remember the words. Sunday school was unique, and I always had a good Sunday school teacher who took the time to share with us the great things about Jesus. Mrs. Smith was my Sunday school teacher, and she was very quiet but was the best teacher. She always brought lollipops for us to eat after the lessons.

After Sunday school, church service would begin, and we had a pastor by the name of Reverend Charlie Martin. He was a big man, with a big family and he always preached hard to the congregation. There were always women who were wearing white dresses with white gloves walking around during church. Ushers as they were called, carried fans around with them and little envelopes and they were quick to get your attention if they heard you mumble a peep during church service. If they observed you chewing gum, that was a major issue, and you might just get escorted outside where you could get scolded. They also controlled when you could enter the church and where you could sit.

Church service was always long, and I could hardly wait to leave. Charlie Martin would always preach about getting saved and not dying and going to hell. I was always afraid that I would die and burn in hell. I always listened to him when he would say "get saved." He would say, "Get baptized so you can wash away your sins and become new." It always stayed with me long after church service that if I were to die that I would go to hell. Each Sunday, there was always someone that I knew that would go to the altar for prayer and then those ladies in white would come whisper in the person's ear and they would then whisper to Rev. Charlie Martin that the person standing at the altar wanted to be saved. It was an amazing and scary process each time I observed it taking place.

Most of the time the person standing at the altar would

turn around and profess to the audience that he or she would like to be baptized and saved. The preacher would say some words to the audience such as "this person has come to the audience asking to be baptized and saved." He would then ask the individual if they would accept Jesus as his or her Lord and Savior and the person would tell the congregation, "Yes." The church members would then proceed to congratulate the new member in Christ. At the conclusion of service, the preacher would tell the audience that our new member in Christ would be baptized next Sunday.

As a young kid, I knew that someday I would do the same thing. In 1985, I accepted Christ as my Lord and Savior and consequently was baptized and accepted into the church as a member in Christ. Mount Pilgrim Baptist Church is still the church my mom and most of my family attend today. Rev. Charlie Martin is no longer the preacher, but new leadership has grown the congregation and new membership.

Chapter Seven

The Day of Aunt Linnie's Passing

After a couple of years of staying with my Aunt Linnie and Pat, I realized those moments were precious and they taught me a lot about family and who I was as a young boy. Aunt Linnie and Pat accepted life for what it was without all the worries of trying to be like those around them. They were unique and were honest people that always had a strong story to tell. I learned that less is better, and honesty is valuable at all times. I also learned to treat people with dignity and respect no matter who they are and to live life to the fullest.

Everything about growing up isn't always exciting. Staying with my Aunt Linnie was the thrill of my life as a young boy. On April 3, 1979, my Aunt Linnie passed on to be with our Lord. Her memorial obituary read as followed:

> Born in Spartanburg County, she was a member of Mt. Pilgrim Baptist Church. Surviving are a sister,

Ambrolas Moore of the home; brothers Louis Moore of Columbus, Ohio, Luther J. Moore of Wellford and James Moore of Lyman. Services will be announced by Sullivan Brothers Mortuary.

I cried and cried when my Aunt Linnie passed away. I didn't understand death at that time and her death was really a hard blow for me. She loved me, fed me, encouraged me, and made me value so many things that most take for granted. Her love was genuine, and she expected that in return. I remember crying uncontrollably at her funeral and feeling the gloom of never being able to see her smile and her concern for my future. I remember imagining how it would feel to visit her wonderful and exciting house and not hearing her soft voice calling for me. I'll never forget her most precious Bible verse:

> *Psalm 23 (KJV): The Lord is my shepherd;*
> *I shall not want. He maketh me to lie down in*
> *green pastures: he leadeth me beside the still*
> *waters. He restoreth my soul: he leadeth me in*
> *the paths of righteousness for his name's sake.*
> *Yea, though I walk through the valley of the*
> *shadow of death, I will fear no evil: for thou*
> *art with me; thy rod and thy staff they comfort*

me. Thou preparest a table before me in the presence of mine enemies: thou anointest my head with oil; my cup runneth over. Surely goodness and mercy shall follow me all the days of my life: and I will dwell in the house of the Lord for ever.

I remember the night after her funeral as I slept, I slightly awoke to see a figure in my room that resembled my Aunt Linnie. I wondered if she was trying to let me know that she was fine and at peace. I assumed that much.

Chapter Eight

The Journey of Bay

U ncle Robert was my mom's youngest brother who was kicked out of his mom's house at sixteen years of age for some unknown reason. My mom and dad persuaded him to move in with us which was super awesome. He would also babysit me sometimes while my mom was working. My Uncle Robert was totally cool! Cool in his style, cool in his cars, cool in his friends, and cool in his assortment of beautiful women.

After my Aunt Linnie passed away, my mom decided to let my Uncle Robert, who was the baby of her family, babysit me. His family nickname was Bay (short for Baby) and he has always been my mom's best friend and greatest support. How strange it was that my uncle would now be sleeping in a bunk bed with me. I was always a scary kid, so having someone sleeping in my upper bunk bed would be great. He always kept me fed and entertained with his collection of music albums and eight track cassettes. Uncle Robert would play his music loud and we would sing some of the songs together. He would often take me to Paces, which was a local restaurant that served the best hot dogs and hamburgers.

Life for me would never be the same because my uncle was showing me so many awesome things. Every Thursday, when he didn't work, we would always watch *The Waltons* TV program. That show always had a moral at the end and I learned many valuable life lessons from watching this show with my favorite uncle on Thursdays.

One morning when I woke up, something had bitten me on my groin area. I wasn't sure what to do because my mom and dad were at work. My uncle kind of panicked, and he wasn't sure how to approach this delicate situation. I recall him calling my mom and she kindly gave him the guidance on how to manage our little situation. He took me to the doctor where they checked me and gave me some Benadryl. Uncle Robert back then was cool and to this day he remains cool. He has always been one of my biggest role models and friend.

Uncle Robert was focused on working and saving his money to do positive things with it. He always kept his car clean on the inside and outside and Saturdays were days for him to wash and shine his cars up. He always had very attractive and smart women around him, and I swore when I grew up that I wanted to be just like my Uncle Robert.

Chapter Nine

Fishing with Big Tom

Uncle Robert wasn't the only great uncle I had. Big Tom was nicknamed Big Tom because he weighed around 340 pounds but could run very fast for his size. Big Tom was the local backyard car repairman and he lived next door to my parents and me. Any time you saw Big Tom his hands were always dark and greasy looking. Most of the local men in the neighborhood hung out in Tom's repair shop.

Sometimes late into the night you could hear Big Tom and others laughing and talking loudly. Tom was a good man and watching him eat anything was absolutely a sight to see. He could chew his food using both jaws. Most normal individuals chew on one side or the other, but Big Tom could put some food away.

Big Tom was also a very good fisherman. He would often take me fishing in local ponds around town. I always enjoyed the quiet sound of leaves rustling and the sound of small waves crashing the banks. Sometimes I would just investigate the sky during slow moments of fishing and marvel at all the grand beauty that God has allowed us to see. Fishing was just an extra for me because the still of the forest was worth everything.

Most of the time, Uncle Tom and I would catch a few here and there. We would always bring my mom whatever we caught so she could fry the fresh fish up for dinner. Sometimes when I was outside playing alone, Big Tom would come into my yard and either throw the football or shoot hoops with me. He was a big kid in a lot of ways, but he made living next door to him the best.

One summer day, while Big Tom was plowing the garden, he had sat his wallet down on the ground, and it had sat there over several days. So, one day as I was playing in the yard, I noticed the wallet and there was over seven hundred dollars in it. I was so excited to find the wallet, so when I returned the wallet to Big Tom, I was anticipating some type of small reward. When I asked my mom about what she thought about him giving me a reward, she simply told me, "Don't get your hopes up too high," but I just knew he would be excited.

So, the day that he came over to the house to get the wallet from my mom he grabbed me and gave me a strong manly hug and handed me twenty dollars. I jumped for joy, because I knew he really didn't have to give me anything. He always protected me whenever he saw that I was doing something silly. Money is a small token when you have concern and love for someone.

Chapter Ten

Dad and His Influence

Dad has been my biggest influence and my life experiences were produced due to the commitment and dedication he provided to giving me the best he had. Dad's story begins at the age of eighteen when he was married at a very young age to my mom. When I was born, he barely had enough money to pay for the discharge fee from the hospital. In order to pay this discharge fee, he had to borrow money from his mother-in-law. Having to borrow money from his mother-in-law made him feel less than a man, at that time. As soon as he was able to earn enough money, he repaid her.

During the time of my birth, my mom and dad had very little, but he made a vow to himself that his family would have a better life than what he had. At the time of my birth, my dad had just started working at Firestone Steel Products. After working on this job for three months, there was a layoff while he was working third shift during the night. He was very afraid that he was going to be laid off because he was the only one working in the household. With luck, he wasn't laid off, but the fear of not being able to provide for the family was just too much, so the next day, he went and found another job.

My dad went and sought employment with Burnette TV and Appliances, but also continued to work at Firestone Steel Products at night. It was at this point that he realized and started to understand the meaning of a dollar. Living from paycheck to paycheck was a struggle. With the income from the second job, his wife opened a savings account. The money from the second job allowed my father the opportunity to purchase a US savings bond in the amount of $18.75 weekly.

Dad continued to work two jobs and save all the money that he could afford to save. My parents lived in an old house with no inside plumbing; however, this was by choice, because he and his wife agreed to sacrifice in order to have a house built by the age of twenty-one. With God's support, they started building their first house two months before his twenty-second birthday. After building their first home and moving in, my parents only had furniture in three of the six rooms. My parents had used all their savings on the down payment of their new home. They also had to focus more on how they used their funding, they even started saving pennies in glass jars. Thirty years later my parents continue to save pennies with several large pickle jars.

While working at Burnette TV and Appliances my dad became interested in learning how to repair appliances. With this goal constantly on his mind, he decided to attend Spartanburg Technical School. He shortly became aware of the entry exam he would have to pass in order to attend technical school. Dad was not the best student in high school; consequently, not taking high school seriously he found himself unable to start technical school because he failed the entrance exam. This setback did not sway my dad, so for him to seek acceptance into the technical school he had to take a six-week refresher class.

Dad enrolled in the refresher course, but with the assistance of a person in the admissions office he was able to retake the admissions test, but this time he would pass the test. He was soon enrolled in his first heating and air conditioning class at technical school and he also began working with Spartan Installations Company. This would allow him the opportunity to receive hands-on training. He worked with this company for three months and began working for Robinson Heating Company. My dad worked for this organization for only two weeks. He was searching for a perfect fit in his goal to become a repairman and had decided that this was his true calling.

One day while he was looking through the yellow pages, he discovered Tyler's Appliance Company, and they were willing to train him while he worked as an employee. My dad worked with this company for several years and during that time my parents had my little sister, Nikki.

Dad started his own business in 1977, and it was called Benson Refrigeration and Appliance Service. So, during this time he continued to work two jobs: Firestone Steel Products and his own appliance business. Many times, people would confuse my dad's last name with Benson Furniture, which was located near my dad's business. My dad's business continued to grow because he advertised and provided quality work.

My dad laid out a foundation for his family based on consistency, determination, and a willingness to make sacrifices. He often says that if he had to do things all over again, he would only do one thing differently, and that would be to have taken his education more seriously when he was in school. He continues to work his appliance business after forty years of superb service. My dad's expectations would go on to follow me on my journey through elementary to the accomplishment of becoming Dr. Thomas L. Benson, III. My dad taught me that nothing is given for free. You work hard and you work to make your life better. Dreams are fine but it's what you do in the day-to-day progressions that makes those dreams a reality.

Chapter Eleven

Birth of Little Sister

My little sister Nikki was born on October 6, and that date will always be considered a special day. Until that date, I was alone with my parents and I would often sit alone watching television and wanting someone to play with. I must be honest, I kind of wished that I had a brother, but when my sister came into the world, we both made the most out of the fun we could share. I remember building castles in the house made of blankets and how we would connect them to furniture so that they would stay in place. We could play for hours in that little cloth house. She was my little sister, the one person that I was glad to have in my life after being the only child for several years.

Even though I was eight years older than my little sister she has always acted like she was the boss. My sister has a strong personality, and most people would call it bossy. But I love her anyway. My mom is considered the number one boss, but if you ask my sister, she will tell you that she's number two. They both have strong personalities, and they possess big hearts for helping those around them. Giving and helping those less fortunate is what makes them extremely special women.

Nikki has grown into a beautiful lady, wife, and mother that I am extremely happy to have as a sister. My sister has always kept me grounded, and even today, she lets me know that I'm just her big brother and that I am nothing for anyone to jump up and down about. Many times, as we were growing up, we have always challenged each other on who our parents loved the most. We have learned that it doesn't matter as long as we love and respect each other. As the older brother, I realize my role is to ensure that our family's legacy continues to flourish and grow. My sister is the matriarch of the family, behind our mother, and when the time comes, we both have roles to play in our family. Love is the power that keeps a family strong, and my sister and I are clear in our roles of how we need to keep our family's legacy solid.

Chapter Twelve

Red Rover, Red Rover into Lyman Elementary

As I turned six years old my journey through elementary school was adventurous, to say the least. I went to Lyman Elementary School from first grade to sixth grade and the experience was joyous, but rooted in discrimination. A term that back then, I had no understanding about. First grade was a challenge because I lacked social skills and lacked comprehension skills. I remember having to read aloud in front of my classmates and struggling to pronounce words and explain the details that I had read.

I was thrust into a remedial resource class for students with learning disabilities and my memory of that transition is one of embarrassment. Embarrassment because I remember having to be singled out of my class by my resource teacher when it was time to work one on one with her. I remember putting my head on my desk whenever I knew she was coming by the classroom to pull me out. How sad and how dejected I felt knowing that everyone in my classroom knew or assumed that I was special and wasn't provided the same type of instructional support that they were receiving. My classmates always stared at me when my resource teacher came to get me. They knew and I knew that I was different, and that difference would stay with me for a very long time.

Mrs. Dennis was my resource teacher, and her main role was to work with me on my pronunciation of words and my comprehension skills. She was a nice lady that took time to know me as a person and as a student. I don't know if she understood how I perceived her approach to getting me out of class for our remediation sessions, but if she did, I would like to think that she would have found a different way of coming to my class. As the only black student in most of my classes through elementary school, I struggled with how to fit into this all-white culture. I remember games like Red Rover, Red Rover and Heads Up, Seven Up.

Red Rover, Red Rover was a game where one group of kids line up about fifty yards apart from another equal number of students facing them and they all connected hand to hand. One student is given the opportunity to say, "Red Rover, Red Rover send [student's name] over," so when that student's name is recognized he/she sprints towards the facing line of students and he/she must attempt to break the grip of two students holding hands. The point that I'm trying to make is that I was never called over, and it hurt me to feel left out. From first grade to sixth grade we played that game and it always made me feel like I didn't matter. Heads Up, Seven Up was a game where all students have their heads lying down on their desk with eyes closed and a student was designated by the teacher to walk around and tap a student on the head. The objective was for the student who was tapped on the head to identify or recognize who had tapped them on the head. I was tapped on the head maybe twice in my years of attending elementary school.

Those experiences made me realize how different I was from all the other white students in my class. How when the topic of any black historical figure came up on any given educational subject, how that cold embarrassing feeling came over me. I was made to feel embarrassed about the many historical figures that have helped our race. I could always see everyone's eyes drift towards me when the word "black" came up. How I felt like the monkey at the zoo that everyone marveled at. The monkey that no one wanted to get close to.

I learned my place and how inferior those around me thought I was, and those experiences at Lyman Elementary were forever life-changing in a negative light. I have always struggled with the norms that are clearly defined by our society as a black person. As black people we always had to assimilate into the norm for us to benefit personally or financially. Even with assimilation, we are still considered less intelligent.

Chapter Thirteen

David The Bull

Bullying in schools happens on a day-to-day basis, so even with my awesome experiences, I experienced racism and bullying. As a black male growing up in an all-white school, I faced discrimination at the water fountain, in the coat room, and out on the playground. I learned how to avoid many situations but there were times when I would face hard lessons, and this was one example. Fifth-grade year started out exciting because I knew the next year would be my last year at Lyman Elementary. My days would go by fast with little issue, except for the day I was in the cafeteria speaking to a group of guys at my lunch table.

David was a white boy with big muscles for a sixth-grader, he also played football and lifted weights. I remember telling the guys at the table that he looked like a bull because he had thick shoulders. So, as the end of school came around, I walked out of the school building and I noticed some of the guys that were sitting with me at the lunch table were circled around the kid, David. As I walked past the group, he called my name and the group of guys circled around me.

David asked me what I said about him and I was hesitant at first. He got in my face and the other guys were jeering him on. I then told him what I had said, at that point David punched me in my stomach and I could barely breathe. I felt my eyes welt up, but before I would let them see me cry, I broke out of the circle and ran across the street to the daycare center where I went every day after school. I learned a valuable lesson about trust that day. No matter who claims to be an associate or friend, always watch what you say about others because some people only want to see you hurt.

Chapter Fourteen

Swimming into New Waters

The summer going into my sixth-grade year was the summer I learned how to swim. That's also when I learned about a man named Coach Cagle. Coach Cagle was a big old white man with a bald head and gray beard. He was the football coach for Lyman Elementary and the swim teacher at Lyman Pool. Lyman Pool was a swimming pool for whites only, but that year was the first year blacks could swim in the segregated pool, and unfortunately, my first time learning how to swim.

My first lesson was terrifying because everyone there was white, and all the parents were standing around the pool watching me like I was a walking disease, and Mr. Cagle didn't make it easier for me. He was very demanding and scary man. I struggled to learn at first because of all the distractions. One day after swim lessons were over, I remember several white boys walking up on my cousin and me. They were pretending to spit in our hair. We told them to stop but it just made them do it more and more.

As I progressed in my swimming lessons, it came to a point where I had my swim test, and that meant that I would have to swim in the ten-foot section of the pool and jump off the high diving board. Mr. Cagle pulled me into the ten-foot-deep section of the pool, and I had to swim from one side of the pool to the other side. I had observed several other kids barely make it out of the ten-foot water. I remember at first going straight to the bottom of the pool and Mr. Cagle grabbing me to save me from drowning, but once I gathered myself, I was able to swim across the pool and back. I then jumped from the high diving board and was able to swim to the side of the pool to finish my swimming class. Racism almost discouraged me out of a fundamental practice of learning how to swim. The moments of having those white parents stare at me made me realize that I was human and deserved the same type of respect and dignity that their children received.

Chapter Fifteen

Overcoming the Odds

Dr. Hill Middle and James F. Byrnes High school were the best years of school. I had more black classmates and more opportunities to see individuals like me. Those black classmates made me feel like I mattered. I became more confident in my own skin. Having attended an all-white elementary school where there were very few students who looked like me or faced the same challenges as I did made the transition to middle school and high school exciting.

I struggled in both middle and high school academically, but my parents, and some caring, supportive, and committed teachers helped me overcome many of my academic setbacks. I recall moments when my mom would have me read a passage or two and as she would ask me questions about what I had read, my mind would be blank. My mom would either pinch me or spank me, and I would do my very best to recall information, but it would never come to me. My mind would go completely blank and I never understood why that would occur. I appreciate my mom for her swift delivery of punishment in accordance with my lack of focus or lack of comprehension. Either way, her methods helped me to overcome those deficiencies. Mrs. Hazel, a seventh-grade English teacher, spent a lot of time trying to teach me to overcome my learning disabilities, along with my mom spanking me when I couldn't recall or focus like I needed to. Mrs. Hazel took the time to analyze my deficiencies in reading, writing, and comprehension and created a plan that helped me correct my learning issues. She was patient and demanding at the same time.

Dr. Bomar was my senior English teacher who worked me beyond my capabilities. This man didn't just push me to be a better student, he demanded that I be better than my expectations for myself. He challenged me to be a better writer and allowed me to see my true capabilities. Most people have great teachers, but this man was extraordinary in every way possible. He made me realize that even though I wasn't a great student that I could still achieve college opportunities. He also made me realize that I was a pretty good writer. Dr. Bomar introduced me to a writing club that was on a local college campus. The experience of visiting a college for a writing competition was an awesome experience for me. Writing allowed me to disappear into a different world and music soothed my spirit and allowed the most magical visions and thoughts to come to my mind.

I recall writing poems to girls that I thought were special, such as an original poem by me titled *Beauty*:

"A ray of beauty she possesses. How does she keep the glare from blinding those around her? Time and time again she changes like the seasons. How does she keep the flare from her stride from staggering those that pass by her? Loving her has made a glob of clay a masterpiece for others to marvel and envy."

I soon realized that with a solid education that I could overcome any challenge or obstacle that came my way. Dr. Bomar refused to allow my deficiencies in learning to keep me from aspiring for professional growth. He demanded excellence from me and took the time to know me as a student and was willing to dedicate as much time as possible helping me be the best student I could possibly be. Academically, I was not prepared for college, and before I could even get my scholarship I had to pass the SATs. That was another big struggle that I would face on my journey to college. I took that SATs more than ten times and it seemed like

I would never achieve a 700, which was the qualifying score. Dr. Bomar committed himself to helping me prepare, and his patience for working with me will always be a memory of great love and support. Most teachers halfway commit to their students, but this man did everything in his power and more to help me achieve my goal. I will forever hold him in high regard as a super educator and friend.

Chapter Sixteen

Friday Nights and New Beginnings

Friday nights were filled with the smell of popcorn, fresh cut grass, and bright lights. Byrnes High School sports were good to me. I played football from the fifth grade through my senior year of high school and believe it or not, I was pretty good. My tenth-grade year I was fortunate enough to get moved up to the varsity team as a wide receiver.

Coach Bo Corne, a legend in the South Carolina high school sports, coached our team to the 1986 State Championship, and I was a member of this State Championship team. We beat Berkeley High School in the stadium of the University of South Carolina at Columbia. I even had the awesome opportunity of playing in that game.

My senior year came, and I was blessed with the exciting opportunity of receiving a football scholarship to play football at Wingate College, a Division II South Atlantic Conference. I recall the day that my mom came to the school, and my anticipation of signing my letter of intent was over-whelming. My high school coach and my new college coach were present for this big sports news event. The *Spartanburg Herald Newspaper* was present with a camera to capture this significant moment. With a snap of the camera, the moment was memorialized, and I cut the news clipping the next day.

I envisioned myself going to school and making a big name for myself but before that would happen, I would need to get my body in collegiate level shape. The summer work-out I received from Wingate was filled with several different skill sets. Building strength and getting my cardio in tip-top shape. Day in and day out, I was spending time working out and eating healthy foods. The demands of college-level football were very demanding and required a full-time commitment on my behalf.

Chapter Seventeen

The Greek Pathway

My second year of college, I had a GPA high enough to pledge during the fall of 1990 at Wingate College. I ventured into the arena of pledging the most distinguished organization of Kappa Alpha Psi Incorporated; this journey would bring me into a bond that would open major doors of opportunity, brotherhood, and lifelong friendships. This journey would bring together eleven young men, all were former or current football players for Wingate College. The order of my fraternity brothers was as followed: Marian Bruce, Leon Anderson, Mike Ragin, Reggie Cannon, myself, Billy Blakney, Appel Gipson, Joe Willis, Robert Mosley, Russell Booker, and Jerry Ratchford. I knew each of these individuals through football, but our journey together would make us brothers for the rest of our lives.

Pledging any fraternity or sorority begins and ends with the history and mission of the organization, but there are so many other things that most people would not imagine. We learned the history, about each other, and working together as one unit. The difficulty is when you only know a few things about the people you're on a journey with, but the expectation is for you to become one. In order to make this journey, everyone must become one, and we all must know everything possible about the individuals on our fraternity line as well as about the organization.

Wingate did not have fraternities or sororities during my time at school. Pledging on a campus without fraternities or sororities is especially difficult because fraternity members from local universities and colleges have free access to visit a campus at any time and make everyone's lives miserable. Our goal was to make sure we were in sync with each other, but with eleven individual minds that was not easy. As we started this journey, we encountered questions, games, and other types of humiliating gags that were meant to challenge us as a group but with the intent of making us grow together as one.

There were nights when other members of the fraternity would come on campus and they would spend hours making our lives as miserable as possible. Sometimes to the point where we were in tears and begging for relief. One night each of us had to eat a gigantic onion and drink a whole bottle of Texas Pete Hot Sauce and chase all of that with mineral oil. That night was the culminating conclusion of six weeks of going through the most intense pledging we had experienced and at this point we were in sync and knew all the knowledge we needed to know about our illustrious fraternity. After six weeks of education and gags, we were prepared to become members of Kappa Alpha Psi Fraternity Incorporated which provided me the opportunity of meeting many distinguished black men like myself and having many doors of opportunity opened for me.

Chapter Eighteen

Exodus out of Kentucky

My whole high school experience was about football and I worked as hard as I could to make that dream come true. I was considered a Red Shirt freshman in college, which meant that I would sit out of practice as a freshman in order to build my academic skill sets. I was guaranteed five years of athletic eligibility and that was going to be a great opportunity for me. My second year of college was a struggle for me because I wasn't doing the best in my academics; however, I was doing very well as an athlete on the football field. I remember our first game was against Kentucky State and we were so excited to be traveling that far for a historically black college football game. We traveled there with the hopes of winning our first game of the season and my goal was to catch as many passes and touchdowns that I could possibly make.

I remember as the game started my fellow receiver got the start for the game which upset me because I knew I had worked extremely hard to start that game. I somewhat had a chip on my shoulder and if I had been smart, I would have released that anger at a different time outside of my football game. When my coach called for me to go into the game it was a play designated for me. The play was eighty-two switch, which called for me to spread wide right, then at the snap of the ball my pass pattern consisted of me running fifteen yards then running a seam pattern toward the middle of the field. As I ran the pattern, the pattern had me wide open right down the middle of the field and the quarterback threw the ball in my direction, but it was high, and it caused me to twist my back backwards to catch the ball. Unfortunately, I missed the ball but what I wasn't expecting was the hit that the free safety would deliver. The tackle severely injured my abdominal area, which had me laying and moaning out in the middle of the football field.

The athletic trainer came to the field to try to help me, but at that moment I knew my life would never be the same. As I was carried off the field, the Kentucky State football team was preparing for halftime and the band was preparing to come onto the field. The band members were trash talking me and calling me names. My trainer had the ambulance transport me to the emergency room where they inserted a drainage tube through my nose and into my stomach to drain blood from my abdominal area. I was not sure what was going on and the doctor was not sure either, but we both knew it was not normal for me to be bleeding internally.

Soon my parents would arrive and transport me from the hospital after I had stayed in there overnight. I was so glad to have such a supportive coach to stay with me until my parents came to my rescue. My mom and dad drove over eight hours to transport me to South Carolina. After several days of recovery, I decided to go back to school to catch up on my work, but for some strange reason I was not able to keep any food on my stomach. Things were not feeling the best with my abdominal area, nor with my energy level, so my athletic trainer made me a referral to an internal doctor.

On the day of my doctor's appointment, one of my close dorm buddies and fraternity brothers rode with me to my appointment. The meeting with my new doctor quickly revealed that I was in bad shape internally and I was immediately placed into the hospital in Carolinas Medical Center in Charlotte. I quickly called my parents to let them know that my doctor had diagnosed me with a torn pancreas that was severely swollen, and they weren't sure how they were going to repair my damaged organ. I cried as I was telling my mom what the doctor had revealed to me. But my mom was very passionate and told me that "we would get through it."

After staying in the hospital six weeks and having

extensive surgery to remove sixty percent of my pancreas, I was going home. I realized my football career was over and I had to withdraw from school for the remainder of the semester. But the President of Wingate, Dr. Jerry McGee, promised me that I would keep my football scholarship, but without having to participate in football. In my heart and mind I cried because the potential dreams of what I would accomplish as an athlete were completely taken away. No more football practices, lifting with my teammates, feeling the intensity of the moment before the game, and the glory of winning and losing. It was forever taken away from me.

I remember walking out of my dorm room and walking to the practice field and just sitting near the practice field and crying silently because something I loved was forever gone. I soon realized after several months that my injury would not stop me from being around sports, so I changed my college major from business to sports medicine. Ruth Haugen, my college athletic trainer, was determined to get me involved in our athletic training team, and it was her motivation that was the catalyst for me to jump headfirst into the sports medicine academic program of study. I knew that my injury would allow me to encourage others who suffered injuries to strive for a successful return to play.

Chapter Nineteen

Mom the Biggest Supporter

During my stay in the hospital from my football injury, my mom had always been my biggest supporter, but it was not until I spent six weeks in the hospital that I realized that my mom was more than special. My mom stayed with me and cared for me during my time in the hospital. There were times when I saw the look of despair in her face when moments were not the best for me. She never cried or showed any type of frustration. Throughout my life, my mom has protected me and fought for my rights as a little black boy in school, sports, and any other area where she felt like I was being mistreated. She's a small woman in stature, but she's strong like a giant with a big heart.

I remember when I was playing football at Lyman Elementary and the players were calling my cousin and me the N-word. It was very bad for the two of us because when we changed in the locker room no adult was present so the older boys would throw things at us and call us the racial slur. Eventually, I told my mom about the situation and the very next day she showed up on the football field and she was not concerned about who was around nor that the coach was a man. She let that coach have it and from that day on no one ever bothered us again. There were so many times that my mom has come to my rescue. I love my mom for all the wonderful things she has done to protect and love me.

Chapter Twenty

Transition into New Changes

After my injury, I began my long transition into a new major; I realized just how God had redirected my path, and it was a path that would cause changes for the better. As I managed to deal with the loss of my athletic participation, I began to understand that athletes around the world deal with catastrophic career ending injuries every day and that mine was no exception. I could still play a big role in sports, and because of my injury, I was well suited to help others manage their injuries and possibly help those who are injured. I remember how much of a struggle it was for me to accept the fact that I was no longer able to participate in collegiate football. I remember moments of walking the campus of Wingate and walking to the practice football field crying my eyes out. I cried because I didn't have a chance to leave the sport that I loved under my own will. God forced this change on me, and it was up to me to manage my new circumstances.

I would never have the opportunity of getting dressed on Saturday in my football uniform with my teammates and having those butterflies during pre-game. Missing the moments when kickoff happens and the call for offense to take the field and lining up at my receiver position to either block or preparing my mind and body for the play call to come to me for a pass route. The anticipation of running my pass route and hitting my target route and waiting for the ball to come my way, making the catch, and doing my best to run towards the endzone for a touchdown. The exhilaration of running into the endzone and having my teammates congratulate me on a well-run pattern, catch, and run for a touchdown. Celebrating the glory of winning a hard-fought game and the love and support provided by the fans after the game. I thought my life would never be the same or at least that's what I thought.

I still have moments where I wish I had worked harder in the weight room and on my conditioning. I wonder how my last two years of college football would have been and if I would have accomplished more achievements and what it would be like to have a second chance at the one pass that I missed that ended my football career. Athletic training/sports medicine was going to be my life and I wanted to be the best athletic trainer I could possibly be, so I studied and practiced my craft with my college classmates. After gaining all the hours of experience and class instruction I was finally ready to graduate from Wingate College with my degree in sports medicine.

Attending the National Athletic Trainers' Association convention in Dallas, Texas, really inspired me even more. Having the opportunity to meet professional athletic trainers from the NFL, NBA, and major university trainers allowed me the opportunity to see myself doing the same thing. That dream would only come first with me passing the National Athletic Trainers Board of Certification Exam, which was a monster of an exam. The exam consisted of a written practical, oral practical, and a simulation exam. The written practical was a standard fifty-question exam; the oral exam consisted of several oral questions and manipulation exercises; and finally, the simulation exam was several real-life simulations of someone being injured and having to make a critical decision about treatment.

My first time taking the exams, I passed the oral and simulation exam, but it would take me several times to pass the written exam; however, on November 12, 1995, I would become a National Board-Certified Athletic Trainer. Obtaining my certification would allow me the opportunity of practicing with a national certification behind me.

I worked several jobs that allowed me the opportunity to practice and refine my skills as an athletic trainer. One new goal that I hoped to attain was working at the college level as a head athletic trainer.

Chapter Twenty-One

Working the HBCU

During the time that I was working at a local high school as a teacher assistant and athletic trainer, I would occasionally drop by Fayetteville State University to talk with their Head Athletic Trainer about the possibility of working with him. A couple of years would pass by before I would finally get my call from the University asking me to interview for the position at the school. I was so prepared and confident about my ability that they hired me on the spot, and I was so excited to be working at the college level. It was all new to me, especially the HBCU experience. Working with ten team sports was a challenge, but I was up for it. The first thing I needed was some student athletic trainers who were interested in possibly becoming certified. I would soon have several students who were consistent with working with the athletic program.

My major sports were football and men/women's basketball. Fall sports would often merge into the winter season so

I would have to put a lot of hours in the training room and traveling. I loved the traveling part of my job. I worked hard and learned a lot about athletic injuries and how empathy makes a difference when working with injured athletes.

Working at Fayetteville State was an eye opener for me due to this being the first time I would experience a culture specifically for black people. My entire life experience had been surrounded by all white people. From elementary school and growing up in rural South Carolina to Wingate College, where the campus was mainly white people, was quite an experience for me. I will always recall the moment I first walked into the cafeteria at Fayetteville State and to observe the beauty of people like myself was exhilarating. Looking at all the beautiful black faces of young women and men made me proud. How amazing things were to see people on a campus socializing and living a simple life without the concerns of racism or discrimination. This small little civilization created on the campus of this HBCU made me relax and feel empowered.

Chapter Twenty-Two

The Power of Lifelong Mentorship

My fraternity brother approached me about joining his mentor group that was held at Max Abbott Middle School. I joined in without any hesitation. I first met Tony in our one-on-one sessions, and we would often talk about his goals and some of the issues he faced on a day-to-day basis. I met Tony as a young thirteen-year-old that was in trouble with the law, at risk of dropping out of school and possibly repeating the same road that he observed his mom take. He was a seventh grader who hated school and anyone in authority. His story from the beginning would have made you question if any of those goals would ever be possible, but the power of a mentorship, if done right, can make all the difference.

My goal was to establish a consistent process by which we could talk openly and honestly with only one exception, and that exception was for him to work hard on his behavior and academic expectations. If he met my expectations rewards would come, and some of those rewards would be attending some of the football and basketball games at Fayetteville State where I was working, and possibly time for him to hang out with me on Saturdays if he met all the expectations. He was hard around the edges and was very defensive about how people viewed him and how he felt like no one believed in him. My conversations at times were about how he could only manage his actions, and if he managed himself better, others like me would be his advocate if he was in the right.

Over time, Tony and I would establish a positive relationship built on honesty and support. I tried to share my life experiences with Tony, such as having him travel with me to visit a family member in New York, participating in my wedding, hanging out on the weekends playing video games, and me spending time at his house with him and his mother. Time made our relationship stronger and I modeled the best behavior I could. He understood that as a grown man that I faced the same types of challenges that he did, except that most of the time I was able to manage my actions, thoughts, and approach to any situation. I often tried to get Tony to become an analytical thinker and to never settle for a simple answer. Tony has become a member of my family and my wife and I view him as our son. Mentoring any individual requires patience, time, commitment, and goals. We never start anything without thinking about a target or particular outcome. Twenty-two years of working with anyone develops a commitment and loyalty that's unbreakable.

Tony Mellon is a thirty-four-year-old man that currently works as a teacher in the Durham Public School System. Most people would see him as a normal to average professional that's just trying to make a difference in the world, but he is way more important than that. Besides working as a former seventh-grade teacher assistant, custodian/bus driver, truck driver, and serving in the Navy, he is a married man with a lovely wife and a new baby on the way. He has been married for five years, and he owns a three-bedroom home that he and his wife worked hard to purchase. He has accomplished many great things thus far. He also works as a mentor to at-risk young men. He has committed his life to serving young people and helping those who need guidance, time, and support. He also shared that same energy and passion with Thomas Benson, IV, my son.

Tony attended Terry Sanford High School, Ramsey Street High Alternative School, Fayetteville Technical School in 2012, where he graduated with his associate degree, the University of North Carolina at Chapel Hill where he graduated in 2014 with a political science degree, and most recently,

North Carolina Central University where he graduated in 2017 with a Master's in Education. The experiences that my dad taught me about being analytical and hardworking allowed me to use those life experiences in a way to mold the life of my young mentee. Taking the time to attend his wrestling matches and football practices gave Tony a support that he desperately desired.

I recall attending one of Tony's football practices, and as I was watching him practice, he slipped on the field and several coaches just ignored him as he lay on the field moaning in pain. So, I yelled at the coaches to let them know that I was Tony's support. They looked at me with astonishment because they were so accustomed to overlooking Tony as they knew he did not have a strong support system. The coaches quickly jumped to Tony's aid. That one moment impacted our relationship forever, and from then on Tony always knew that I was there to support him. The goal now is for me to continue supporting Tony, his wife, and their new baby in their continued journey of living the life he has chosen to live.

Little does Tony know how he contributed to my healing from losing my son, Christian. As I reflect on the time spent with Tony, he was in my life before I met my beautiful wife, in my wedding, at the funeral of my son, and in every major event of my life. He has taught me how to be a parent and he allowed me to share my beliefs and values with him. He allowed me to be his father, and for that I owe him so much more than what I have given to him. I constantly refer to him as my son; I shed tears often when I think about how he was when I first met him and how our relationship has given him salvation from a life of destruction. God knew that I needed support, and for so many years I poured my heart and energy into his life.

I pray that God continues to bless him on his continued journey. My blessing is that I live forever through him, my son, and my beautiful daughter. Merriam-Webster's Dictionary defines "legacy" as something transmitted by or received from an ancestor or predecessor or the past. I have tried to be a model for him in every area of my life. He has seen me at my best and my worst; however, he still respects me, and I would say he loves me as I love him.

Chapter Twenty-Three

Chelle the Chocolate Barbie Doll

During my time of working as the Head Athletic Trainer at Fayetteville State University, I met a beautiful brown-skinned, pretty lady requesting assistance for an injury that she sustained from dancing or stepping. I remember getting a heating pad with a towel to place on her hamstring. I told her to let that sit for twenty minutes and I would remove it, and let her know if her injury didn't get any better, she could come back for more treatment. Later that week, she returned, and we began to make little conversation. We later exchanged phone numbers and we soon began to date.

I did not know that later that lady would become my wife. Life throws curve balls and all you can do is stand in there and hope for the best. My life up to that point was all about my job as an athletic trainer and working with my mentee, Tony. Chelle came into my life at the perfect time because we became friends, and she became someone that I could communicate with and laugh with.

Chelle is eight years younger than me, but I think the age difference allowed us to be patient with each other and contributed to our great chemistry. I remember us sharing trips to Florida and horseback riding. Her excitement for the small things made her special to me. Most men, I guess, look for certain things in a woman, but what I found was a woman that I considered to be REAL. Real in the sense that I could always be myself.

On July 13, 2002, she made me the proudest man in the world. She would also grant me the opportunity of becoming a DAD to two beautiful kids. Marrying Chelle allowed me the opportunity of joining a wonderful family with a super father-in-law, mother-in-law, several brothers-in-law, and several sisters-in-law. We enjoy our family time together during most holidays and it's always special. Her family, from the beginning, embraced me and loved me like I was a member of the family.

She guided and supported me through two masters', and my doctoral degree. We have obtained a beautiful home and a beach condo in North Myrtle Beach, and many marvelous memories. We have been married eighteen years and we are living the dream. She continues to build me up and encourage me. Marriage has taught me that people must be willing to share a lot of themselves but still find the time and space to keep a part of themselves. Meaning both people must create opportunities to have separate time and space for their own growth.

Love and financial wealth can make things flow so much better when two individuals are striving for the same goals.

Chapter Twenty-Four

My Eternal Blessings

Thomas, IV, and Hailey Benson are my jewels and my heart. March 4, 2003, and June 2, 2008, those two dates will forever be engraved in my mind and heart. Those were the dates when I was blessed with my two beautiful kids. Thomas is a handsome, strong, and intelligent young man that will change the future. He has a commitment that's unheard of for a young man at the age of seventeen. He aspires to become a neurosurgeon and ever since he was the age of six or seven, he has told us that he planned to become a great surgeon.

Hailey is my beautiful, passionate, and sensitive daughter that loves to dance and communicate with everyone she encounters. She has a fire and spirit that makes her unstoppable. Watching her dance tinkles my heart because it's so unbelievable that God has given me such a beautiful angel. Daughters are always special to their fathers and my little girl has me wrapped around her finger.

In 2006, my wife and I lost our son Christian Isaiah Benson at birth, and there is not a day that goes by that we don't have moments of deep sorrow. Losing a child changed me in ways that I never realized until years later.

Chapter Twenty-Five

Losing Christian

Expecting parents have so many emotional moments that they experience during pregnancy. My wife and I were so excited when we found out that we were having another son. We had our son Thomas, but we had so many emotions about having another boy in our family. My wife and I did everything her doctor required her to do during her pregnancy, and for the most part things were easy.

It was during the last trimester of my wife's pregnancy that she began to experience a cold and it had her bed ridden, which for my wife never happens so I knew something was wrong, but unfortunately it was the weekend and her doctor's office was closed. She called her doctor's office and they communicated to her that she should take basic cold medicine. My wife's water broke, so at that point, we rushed to the hospital. I will never forget getting dressed in my hospital gown and the doctor preparing my wife for the delivery of our son, Christian.

As the doctor began the procedure to deliver our baby, I was holding my wife's hand, and it was at this moment that the doctor pulled the baby from my wife's belly, but there was a deafly sound. The doctor laid our baby on a medical table far from my wife and me. I recall my wife looking at me and asking me how's the baby. I looked at the doctor and he came over to us and said that Christian didn't survive. I dropped to the floor with astonishment and something in my mind told me to be strong for my wife, so I did my best to stay strong for her. My wife and I cried together, and the doctor allowed us the opportunity of holding our deceased baby. The doctor took special attention to my wife because her blood pressure was extremely high, and they were concerned about her health.

So, planning our baby's funeral was something that I never planned, but with the assistance of my supportive family I was able to accomplish this task. I recall calling my dad and him telling me to be strong for my wife and family. I wanted to cry and grieve but I needed to make sure my wife and family were well taken care of, so I stayed strong and followed through on my role. Parents who lose their babies at birth suffer so many psychological issues. We have the hopes and dreams of our new baby, and when that hope is tragically taken away the parents lose a part of themselves that can never be returned.

Every year on the date of July 27, we mourn the loss of our beautiful son. We celebrate his birth as a family and each year place flowers on his headstone at the cemetery. When parents lose a child, it's like a part of you dies. We always anticipate the possibilities of a new baby and all the prospects that come along with it, so losing a child forever haunts those who lose their babies. We planted a tree in honor of our son, and each day I marvel at that tree and the growth that it has shown over the years. I keep it close to the house and when we left our first home, my wife and I dug it up and transported it with us.

My son Christian would be fourteen years old at this point and I often wonder what he thinks of me as his father. If he feel lucky that we are his parents and whether he laughs at our silly moments. I miss him daily. Years have passed since that terrible moment; however, I still suffer deep anguish and sorrow from my loss. I never had my moment to grieve and yell about the loss of my handsome son, so seeking therapy has allowed me to bring to the surface my deep sorrow and how to manage my grief. The concept of a man doesn't cry and that we should be tough has always dominated my life, and I think living by that motto has made me a nutshell.

Chapter Twenty-Six

Journey II
Administration

In 2002, I began the transition of changing careers. For ten years, I had served as a head athletic trainer at Fayetteville State University and as a Duke Basketball Summer Camp Trainer, along with working as a summer soccer trainer at different camps around the state. I had made great friends and great money, but with a family I needed to be home, and I was looking for more income. So, during the time while I was working at Fayetteville State, I completed my Master of Education in middle-grade science along with obtaining my teacher licensure. I worked as a middle-grade science teacher and athletic trainer at Westover Middle School for two years. I then taught at Seventy-First High School where I taught nineth-grade science and worked as the athletic trainer.

After three years in the classroom, I decided to jump into school administration. I was fortunate to be employed at Jack Britt High School as an assistant principal, so I went back to school to obtain my Master of School Administration from the University of North Carolina at Pembroke. What an exciting time it was sharing thoughts and experience with my colleagues about my experiences as an assistant principal/athletic director. I would then accept the challenge of working at two different high schools as an assistant principal, Pine Forest and Hoke High School. Both schools were drastically different with unique issues but with super great students.

Transitioning into school administration allowed me to use my upbringing and life experiences in a way to mold the young lives of students who desperately needed more support. I was able to mold teachers into compassionate caring educators. Taking the time to know each student allows teachers to establish a heartfelt connection that kids can clearly feel and understand. Every student should have a Dr. Bomar as a teacher and possess all the energy and passion that he had. Many teachers bring their personal biases to the classroom and those biases hinder them from focusing on the many facets of serving in the role of an educator. Curricular changes must occur at the college and university level for teachers to be trained in understanding the social and emotional issues that students bring to the classroom and how those needs must be met first before the instructional pedagogy can begin.

Chapter Twenty-Seven

Leadership Through Alternative School

During the time that I was serving as an Assistant Principal at Hoke High, the superintendent asked me to serve as the Interim Principal of Turlington Alternative School which served students in grades sixth through twelfth who were removed from their schools for disciplinary infractions. Some of those students needed guidance, discipline, and in some cases, love. At the conclusion of the school year, I was given the Principalship of J.W. Turlington Alternative School. My goal at the school was to turn it into one where students who were struggling in the traditional setting could find a school that offered them a safe place for learning and finding themselves. I took advantage of all the things my students and teachers showed me about themselves and this thing called school.

My objective was to change the mindset of my teachers so that they could see themselves differently and with hope, and begin to realize the value in themselves and what they provided to students. So many times, teachers are broken themselves, from life or from bad experiences, so my job was to teach them how to value themselves through daily communication and professional development. If teachers feel valued and loved, the hope was that they would make the students feel the same thing. The alternative school allowed me to try many unique things that were positive for students. Like a level system for them to work their way out of the school and back to their traditional school, plus the opportunity for them to be treated like the wonderful students they were. Students could earn privileges like candy, food, and the awesome opportunity of not having to wear the mandated uniform.

During my time at the school, I saw teachers and students transform into superb individuals that had high aspirations. A leader is someone who can take people to a place that they never thought they could possibly attain, and my school was a different school. Unfortunately, I had to leave the school because with success other opportunities come to the forefront. This role was especially special to me because it allowed me the opportunity of helping students who were at risk and broken.

The focus was on training teachers on how to be compassionate and empathetic to students with learning disabilities and students for the most part, below grade level. As someone who was a young kid with my own learning disabilities, it is very important to know what things inhibit kids from learning and developing. The only way a teacher can begin to know those things is by taking the time to personally connect to their students through dialogue and time. Dialogue through daily personal conversations and time through the day-to-day rituals of school and outside events.

Chapter Twenty-Eight

Becoming the Educational Leader

After leaving J. W. Turlington, I would go on to serve principalships at Spring Lake Middle and Westover High School. I would also have the opportunity of serving as the Assistant Superintendent of Human Resource, Child Nutrition, and Transportation. The whole time changing the lives of teachers and students and leaving my mark as an educational leader. I currently serve as a Federal Program Administrator for the North Carolina Department of Public Instruction with the Federal Program Monitoring and Support Division which supports approximately $514,000,000 in federal funds provided to districts and schools each year. The primary role of our division is to provide grants administration, program monitoring, data collection and reporting, and to facilitate the necessary technical assistance to ensure not only compliance, but quality programs for students in the state of North Carolina. Compliance is the first step toward program quality; monitoring is the springboard to providing technical assistance. My secondary responsibility with the division is to serve as the State Coordinator for Neglected or Delinquent.

Having suffered personal loss, working with at-risk students, developing empathy for injured athletes, and serving as a school administrator allowed me to hone all my personal experiences; consequently, providing me with relevant connections that have made me a strong educational leader. In my role, I share those experiences with future and practicing administrators so that they can truly understand the very important and impactful role that play in our educational institutions. There is no other special feeling greater than when you walk into an auditorium full of teachers and students who are there to hear your expectations for the school year. It is empowering to know that you can guide students through some of the ups and downs that they will experience during their time in school. The time when you can encourage and motivate all teachers and students about why the mission for the school year is so important. Letting your students know why they come to school and what role we play as educators in their education.

That message should always be profound and well planned because you only get one opportunity to show your students and teachers who you are as the leader of their school. I compare that feeling to a head coach of a sport and how they get their players motivated to play. Educational leaders must be willing to craft a message of empowerment for the students and teachers for them to stay motivated to the mission. Every day the message must be communicated to ensure that everyone understands their role.

Chapter Twenty-Nine

That Sweet Sound
of Dr. Benson

O ne goal that I did not think would ever happen was the opportunity to start my doctoral degree. As I reflect on where I started, it's amazing how God works in all of us. From a student with a major speech impediment, comprehension issues, and a student reading below grade level, I had made the impossible, possible. God made it possible. When I first started my doctoral classes I started at The University of North Carolina at Greensboro with two courses. Driving from work in Fayetteville to Greensboro was a challenge twice out of the week, but I did it because it was going to be worth it. At the end of the spring semester, I finished with two A's and there were more to come.

I was told in the fall that Wingate University would have a cohort program and the classes were on Saturdays from 9 a.m. till 4 p.m., with two classes. Summer classes were also part of the requirements where four classes were offered. I applied to the program and with the blessing of God, I was accepted in and my journey to become Dr. Thomas Benson would begin. I tried to transfer the two courses that I had taken, but Wingate would not allow me to transfer those courses. Saturday after Saturday, I attended Wingate working on papers and presenting information about education and all of its aspects. The experience was like a long marathon and I would not give up. Working with the cohort members of my doctoral studies was the highlight of my experiences of obtaining my degree. I gained valuable knowledge and lifelong friendships with my colleagues.

On December of 2011, I achieved my Superintendent licensure and the next level of my quest was to finish the doctoral degree. After many heartaches and ups and downs, I finally defended my dissertation on October 3, 2013, with my wife present to celebrate my major accomplishment. I participated in my graduation ceremony on May 2013, and what a moment it was for me to finally achieve a lifelong dream. Looking back on where I came from, many of my friends and family didn't even believe in me. Some of them even said I would never make it. But I made it anyway! When I reflect on the young kid who was removed from class for remediation, while all my classmates looked at me as if I was strange, and the many times my mom sat with me frustrated by my lack of comprehension, I marvel at how my life, even with all the setbacks, has turned out. Obtaining my undergraduate, two master's degrees, and a doctoral degree should encourage anyone with any type of obstacle to continue to work hard.

Chapter Thirty

Inner Battles Within My Mind

When do you realize you've made it, but you're left with crazy thoughts? As a man with four degrees, a beautiful wife and family, beautiful home and beach condo, and a super job, why do I find myself unhappy? For a long time, I wasn't sure why I wasn't happy until I sought help from a therapist. People will have all the money they need to survive but still find themselves unhappy. I once looked upon those people as if they were crazy, but the more you achieve and accomplish, in most cases, the less likely you are to be happy. Battling with anxiety and depression isn't what most people would consider successful, but here I am battling something that I'm not familiar with.

For years, you look at those around you, and you envy them, but when you achieve personal goals and still find yourself unhappy, what do you do? After seeking guidance from a therapist, I am slowly learning how to manage my thoughts. The mind is an amazing organ and even though I have so many great things to celebrate and be happy about, I find myself trying to fix me. With my crazy life and all the things that I have experienced, I have guarded my thoughts and feelings for so long that it has caused me many health issues. As we grow into adults and we begin to achieve our dreams, how do we continue to find our own inner happiness?

To those who are reading this book, make sure you take the time along the journey to appreciate those around you that you encounter and find the time to appreciate the person that you are. The educational achievements are great but what good are they when you can't completely be happy with the new person you have grown into? I think you also have to realize that those closest to you change because you sacrifice so much that at the end of your journey, you realize that you have left a part of those you once knew in the past. Therefore, you must rediscover those individuals and begin to learn about them again.

Most people look happy and content from a distance, but if you really look deeper within their personal lives they're most likely dealing with some type of mental issue. The key to managing all of that is seeking counseling or therapy. It has helped me to see my weaknesses and with time I plan to rise above those anxieties and moments of depression. As an educator, I realize that I suffered from a form of dyslexia, and my traumatic experiences throughout my upbringing and life have caused many of the psychological issues that I face. Discrimination, bullying, racism, personal injury, and the loss of my son have drastically impacted my mind.

The unique thing about seeking help is that it allows you to see things in black and white. The tragedy of things experienced have made my life a little chaotic. Chaotic in a good and bad way. Good because it has made me the person that I am today and bad because I carry so many negative things around with me. No person has a perfect life and those experiences in some form or fashion stay with an individual for a very long time, even when you don't realize it. Therapy allows you the opportunity to bring out, through conversation, the obstacles that have impacted you, and hopefully allows you to face those issues through analytical prioritization. Prioritizing those things that have kept you from moving forward and those things that you need to let go of.

Chapter Thirty-One

The Legacy Created

This book is inspired by my personal experiences growing up in Lyman, South Carolina. I hope this book serves to inspire young and older adults about a time when life was slow and little things meant a great deal. Merriam-Webster defines "legacy" as "something transmitted or received from an ancestor or predecessor." My journey and experiences will guide you through a life filled with challenges, and all the memories have encouraged me to look back with pride.

For you, this book will inspire courage, and a tenacity to look for a silver lining in success. Whether it's family or close friendships in your community, there will be defining moments that will inspire your journey. I am a former educator/administrator in our public-school system, and I currently serve as a Federal Program Administrator with the North Carolina Department of Public Instruction. I genuinely believe that my personal experiences and educational journey can inspire young people and old about the importance of appreciating every moment of our youth and never taking for granted the lessons of life.

Reflecting on the little boy who was afraid to leave his mom, to the man who has transitioned from a National Board-Certified Athletic Trainer to a School Administrator, Assistant Superintendent, then to a Federal Program Administrator working at the North Carolina Department of Public Instruction, God has held my hand along the way. My story along with my dad's resiliency of never giving up, never quitting, and a no surrender mindset has allowed me to overcome a learning disability, discrimination, setbacks, and racism. My dad modeled for me what the strength of a man can overcome when he sets his mind to a task. So, I marvel at the thought of my son, Thomas Lee Benson, IV, and how far he will go in his journey. Because we do not go gently into the night!

—Dr. Thomas L. Benson III

Dr. Thomas L. Benson III

D r. Thomas Benson III grew up in the small town of Lyman, South Carolina, in the seventies, spending his childhood years on his aunts' farm. He has received a master's degree from both Fayetteville State University and The University of North Carolina at Pembroke, followed by a doctoral degree from Wingate University. Dr. Benson is a dynamic educator of many years and mentors young adults through establishing meaningful relationships and sharing his life experiences. He currently lives in Raeford, North Carolina, with his wife, son, and daughter.

Lightning Source UK Ltd.
Milton Keynes UK
UKHW011402021121
393256UK00003B/884

9 780578 890036